Metal

Claire Llewellyn

W
FRANKLIN WATTS
LONDON · SYDNEY

First published in 2004
by Franklin Watts
96 Leonard Street
London EC2A 4XD

Franklin Watts Australia
45-51 Huntley Street
Alexandria, NSW 2015

Text copyright © Claire Llewellyn 2004
Design and concept © Franklin Watts 2004

Series advisor: Gill Matthews, non-fiction literacy consultant
and Inset trainer
Editor: Rachel Cooke
Series design: Peter Scoulding
Designer: James Marks
Photography: Ray Moller unless otherwise credited
Acknowledgements: AKG Images: 14bl. T. Campbell/Art Directors/Trip: 19. John Deere: 1, 7t.
Mark Edwards/Still Pictures: 20, 23tr. John Farmer/Art Directors/Trip: 21b. Image Works/Topham:
8, 17t.Bryan Pickering/Eye Ubiquitous: 6. D. Saunders/Art Directors/Trip: 18.

A CIP catalogue record for this book is available from the British Library.

ISBN: 0 7496 5720 0

Printed in Malaysia

Contents

Metal is useful

Metal is a very useful material. It is used to make all sorts of things.

▶ *These things are all made of metal.*

Goblet

Can

Knife, fork and spoon

Saucepan

Can you think
of three other
things that
are made
of metal?

Pen

Keys

Scissors

Paperclips

5

Metal is strong

Metal is hard and strong.
It is used to make buildings and machines.

▶ *Metal trains travel across this strong, metal bridge.*

6

▲ A metal tractor is very useful on the farm.

Have a look around your home. Which machines are made of metal?

▶ This metal scooter is small but strong.

Metal can be sharp

Some metal tools have thin, sharp edges. They are very good for cutting things.

Always take care with sharp tools. They can cut you.

▶ *We chop wood with an axe.*

We cut our hair with scissors.

We cut food with a sharp, metal knife.

Try eating with a metal knife and fork – then with ones made of plastic. Which are better? Why?

9

Metal warms up quickly

Metal things warm up quickly. They are used for cooking and heating.

◄ *Food cooks well in metal pots and pans.*

Take care with very hot things. They can burn you.

Plate

Why do you think the material used to make the iron's handle is plastic not metal?

An iron's plate is made of metal. It gets very hot.

Some metals are magnetic

Some metals stick to magnets. They are magnetic.

▶ Magnets stick to the metal door of this fridge.

These metal paperclips are magnetic. They are being pulled towards the magnet.

Make a collection of pins, coins and other small metal things. Now test them with a magnet. Which are magnetic? Which are not?

Some metals are precious

Gold and silver are precious metals.
They are used to make special things.

Gold crown

Gold ring

Silver cup

Is anything in your home made of gold or silver?

Silver spoon

Silver bracelets

15

Shiny or rusty?

Metal looks shiny when it is clean, but it can go rusty.

► *This kettle is made of metal. It shines when it is clean.*

Cars have metal frames.
Paint stops them rusting.
When some cars get old, the
paint peels off and
they go rusty.

▽ *These metal shears have been left out in the rain. They have gone rusty.*

17

Metal is dug out of the ground

Most metal is found inside rocks. We heat the rocks to take out the metal.

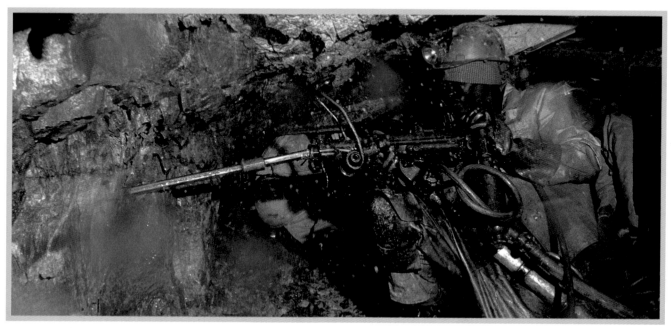

▲ *The rocks are dug out of the ground.*

The rocks are put in a very hot oven. The metal inside them melts. We can pour it out and use it.

Old metal can be melted and used again. This is called recycling.

Shaping metal

Metal is easy to shape when it is hot and soft.

Hot, runny metal is put into a mould.

Metal gets hard when it cools. It keeps the shape of the mould.

This man is hammering hot metal to make a horseshoe.

A person who shapes horseshoes and other metal things is called a blacksmith.

I know that...

1 Metal is useful.

2 Metal is strong.

3 Metal can be sharp.

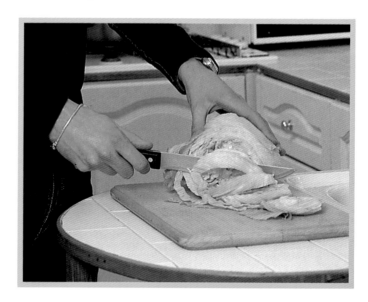

4 Metal warms up quickly.

5 Some metals are magnetic.

6 Some metals are precious.

7 Metal looks shiny when it is clean, but it can go rusty.

8 Metal is found in rocks in the ground.

9 The rocks are heated to take out the metal.

10 Metal is shaped when it is hot and soft. It gets hard again when it is cool.

Index

About this book

I Know That! is designed to introduce children to the process of gathering information and using reference books, one of the key skills needed to begin more formal learning at school. For this reason, each book's structure reflects the information books children will use later in their learning career – with key information in the main text and additional facts and ideas in the captions. The panels give an opportunity for further activities, ideas or discussions. The contents page and index are helpful reference guides.

The language is carefully chosen to be accessible to children just beginning to read. Illustrations support the text but also give information in their own right; active consideration and discussion of images is another key referencing skill. The main aim of the series is to build confidence – showing children how much they already know and giving them the ability to gather new information for themselves. With this in mind, the *I know that...* section at the end of the book is a simple way for children to revisit what they already know as well as what they have learnt from reading the book.